WHAT ABOUT ME?

And 49 Other Surefire Ways to Lose Your Joy

JOYCE MEYER

"Ever find yourself saying these things?
They're joy stealers.
They all stem from an attitude that
can't get past 'What about me?'
They're stinkin' thinkin'. . .poison for your soul."

—Joyce

Secret "Insider" Information

"Why does my life have to be so hard?
Nobody cares about me."

God told me, "Joyce, you can be
pitiful or powerful
but you can't be both."

— NEGATIVE THOUGHT
(boo!)

POSITIVE REACTION +
(hooray!)

Ok, so it's not really a "secret," but now that you're ready to read, it's important
to know that this book is equipped with some very special learning tools.

To assist you in discovering how to dig deeper into your thought life, every two-page spread
is designed with a **negative** (stinkin' thinkin') quote on the <u>left side</u> and a **positive** quote
from Joyce, inspired by God's Word, on the <u>right side</u>, to counteract that negative thought.

Wow! That's a surefire way to learn how to keep your joy!

Over the years as I've taught and shared, I've used honest and sometimes funny little phrases and sayings inspired by God's Word to connect people to the lessons being shared. Most of the time, these phrases have been things that I've felt like the Lord has used in my own life to get my attention off of my own problems in order to get me focused on Him. Some of you may even be familiar with many of these sayings if you've heard me use them during one of my conferences or on the television program *Enjoying Everyday Life*. They are the antidote to acidic, negative thoughts and words that remind me how to stay on track with God's plan for my life.

The title of this book, *What About Me?*, is just one negative thought that has a way of getting into your head and then into your heart, becoming a poison to your soul. It's the type of thought that keeps you focused on yourself and your needs above the needs of others. I've found that thoughts like this are "joy stealers."

We've designed this book to be fun and add joy to your life by giving you helpful, thought-provoking, God-inspired thoughts to counteract negative, cynical, joy-stealing thoughts. My prayer is that you'll find freedom to control your thought life and the ability to walk in a greater measure of joy and happiness in your everyday life.

"What's the big deal? Everybody worries about stuff. It's part of life."

Worry is like a rocking chair...

always in motion, but not going anywhere.

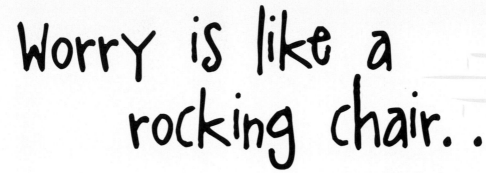

"I don't understand why I can't break this bad habit. . .
it's so hard to change
and I don't want to be like this."

Discipline enables you to think first and act second.

"I try to read the Bible every now and then when I get the chance. I'm just not a very big reader."

Anything you don't feed dies.

We need to take time to feed ourselves spiritually.

"I don't need to tell anyone what I'm really thinking or feeling . . . it's nobody's business but mine."

If you want to get free, you have to first get honest.

"Why aren't things getting better in my life?"

"What we do in the natural doesn't matter;
it's all about being spiritual.
Let me tell you,
the devil knows who I am."

You can't have authority over the devil if you don't have authority over a sink full of dirty dishes.

"That's fine for other people, but I've been through too much."

Nobody has to let their past affect their future.

"I wish I had her life and could do what she does."

People want what someone else has but don't want to go through what they went through to get it.

Your future has no place
for the REGRETS of your past.

"God would never use me.
I'm not smart enough, talented enough or spiritual enough."

"Nothing good ever comes from my problems."

God gives us a double blessing for our trouble.

"I know I don't ever really pray or read my Bible, but I can't figure out why God won't use me to do great things!"

You can't have the perks without the works.

"If God's called me to greatness and He has a great plan for my life, why am I stuck in this job?"

Your **WHO** is not based on Your **DO**.
Your **WHO** is based on **WHO** He says You are. . .

"I WILL NOT forgive that person
until they admit what they did was wrong!"

Do **Yourself** a favor and **forgive.**

"This is how it's always been.
It's never going to get any better.
I'm going to be stuck like this the rest of my life."

"Why does everything good always happen to her? It's SO not fair!"

You can tell how spiritually mature you are when somebody else gets blessed with something you want.

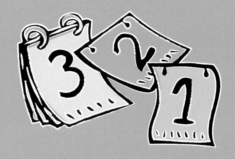

"How long is this going to take?!
I've been waiting TWO WEEKS for
God to get me out of this situation!"

There's no such thing as a drive-through breakthrough.
There's no such thing as microwave maturity.

"I wish I had better relationships, a better job, a better house and just a better life altogether."

Stop wishing and start pressing.

You don't need a wishbone—You need a backbone!

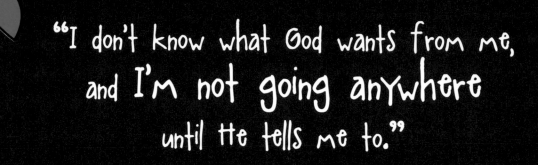

"I don't know what God wants from me, and I'm not going anywhere until He tells me to."

You need to be moving
if you want God to show you which way to go.

"When God explains that to me, then I'll get serious about my relationship with Him."

Faith always has unanswered questions.

hello?

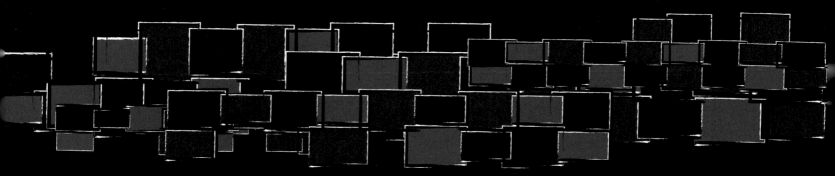

"I don't get it. It seems like every time I pray, God never answers me."

There are no unanswered prayers.

God either says "Yes," "no" or "wait."

"I'm not talking to you again
until you admit you were wrong and I was right!"

When you walk in love,

You give up your right to be right.

"I'm fine. I don't need to change."

"All that stuff works for other people, but God doesn't know what to do with me!"

You're no surprise to God.

He knew what He was getting when He made You.

"I'm basically a good person. . . .most of the time."

You never really know yourself until you see yourself
under pressure.

"It's all my fault—
if I tried harder or had more faith, I know
I'd see miracles or experience something great in my life."

It's your responsibility

to do what God told you to do. . . .
not to worry about the outcome!

"I'm always taking care of everyone and everything else. What about me?"

It is impossible for you to be happy if
you won't get yourself off your mind
and start reaching out to help someone else.

"Why is this happening to me?!
God must be punishing me—
maybe He doesn't really love me or even like me!"

When nothing in your life makes sense,
trust God anyway.

"I've already tried praying and nothing happened!"

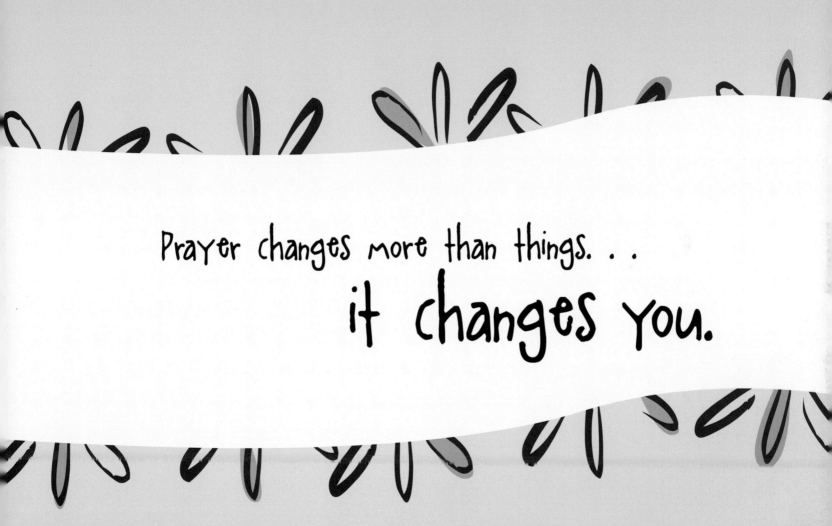

"Most days I feel like nobody even cares how difficult my life is. If only somebody would encourage me, things would be so much better."

When you feel down, go be a blessing
to somebody else.

"I'm so sick of these stupid challenges.
I just wish my life was easy."

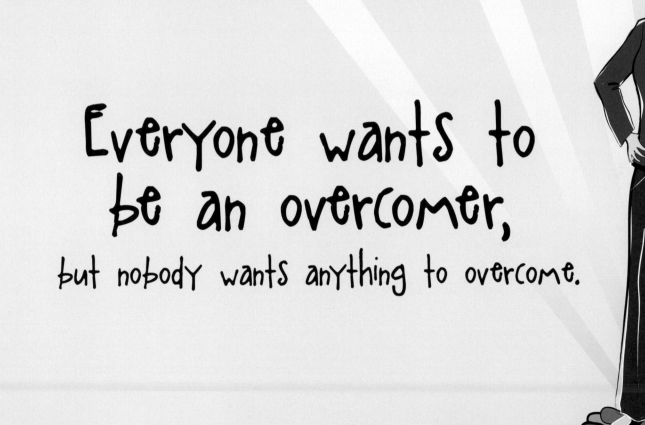

You'll never get up on the outside until you
get up on the inside.

"I really need to put my time in with God today so He will be pleased with me."

We're not doing God a favor by praying each day.

We are doing ourselves the favor.

"I feel like God's so far away.
I wonder if He's forgotten about me,
if He knows what I'm going through,
or if He's got a plan for my life."

God not only sees where you are,

He sees where you can be.

"I don't want to be meek. I'm not a doormat. Why should I let everybody else walk all over me?"

Meekness is not weakness; it's strength under control.

"I'm not confident enough
to do something great for God—
I don't like showing off and telling everybody how great I am."

Real confidence is faith activated.

It is faith taking a step against fear.

Aren't you glad He's the God of "more than enough" and not the God of "barely get by"?

"Nobody cares about me.
I guess no one will ever love me."

self-pity is idolatry.

It's focusing on yourself and idolizing yourself.

"Why does my life have to be so hard?
Nobody cares about me."

God told me, "Joyce, you can be **pitiful or powerful** but you can't be both."

"I've been trying and trying
and nothing ever changes!"

I may not be
where I want to be,
but thank God I'm not where I used to be!

"Someday I'm gonna get rid of this crummy car and this dump of an apartment. I CANNOT wait."

Enjoy where you are

on your way to where you are going.

"If I could just find someone who'd love me then I would be happy."

Don't wait until everything is **perfect** before you decide to enjoy your life.

"I'm not hurting anybody.
God understands I have needs."

Walk with God and **run** from evil.

"I don't trust easily—
God's got to meet me halfway.
When He proves Himself, then I'll trust Him."

You can decide to trust God

or

You can decide to be miserable.

"It's so frustrating dealing with those people! I'm so glad I don't have any junk in my life."

God uses the **junk** in other people to pull the **junk** out of you.

"I know she could really use some encouragement, but she hurt me. If she apologizes then I'll tell her how much I care about her."

People can't see what's in your heart—
they can only see what you do.

"I know what I like and I know what's best for me. Don't worry—I pray every once in a while and ask God if He's got a problem with what I'm doing."

"I can't believe how stupid I was! No matter what I do, I don't think I'll ever be able to make up for that mistake."

Don't mourn bad decisions—

overcome them with good ones.

"I'm really busy right now,
but I'd love to help when I get a chance."

Indifference makes an excuse, but **love** finds a way.

ABOUT THE AUTHOR

JOYCE MEYER is one of the world's leading practical Bible teachers. A #1 New York Times bestselling author, she has written more than ninety inspirational books, including *Power Thoughts*, *The Love Revolution*, *Never Give Up!*, the entire *Battlefield of the Mind* family of books, and two novels, *The Penny* and *Any Minute*, as well as many others. She has also released thousands of audio teachings, as well as a complete video library. Joyce's *Enjoying Everyday Life*® radio and television programs are broadcast around the world, and she travels extensively conducting conferences. Joyce and her husband, Dave, are the parents of four grown children and make their home in St. Louis, Missouri.

JOYCE MEYER MINISTRIES U.S. & FOREIGN OFFICE ADDRESSES

Joyce Meyer Ministries
P.O. Box 655
Fenton, MO 63026
USA
(636) 349-0303
www.joycemeyer.org

Joyce Meyer Ministries—Canada
P.O. Box 7700
Vancouver, BC V6B 4E2
Canada
(800) 868-1002

Joyce Meyer Ministries—Australia
Locked Bag 77
Mansfield Delivery Centre
Queensland 4122
Australia
(07) 3349 1200

Joyce Meyer Ministries—England
P.O. Box 1549
Windsor SL4 1GT
United Kingdom
01753 831102

Joyce Meyer Ministries—South Africa
P.O. Box 5
Cape Town 8000
South Africa
(27) 21-701-1056

Publications by Joyce Meyer ————————————————————————————————

Living Beyond Your Feelings

Never Give Up!

The Confident Woman Devotional

Power Thoughts

Eat the Cookie...Buy the Shoes

The Confident Woman

Hearing from God Each Morning

The Everyday Life Bible

Straight Talk on Fear

The Love Revolution

The Secret to True Happiness

Look Great, Feel Great

Battlefield of the Mind

Approval Addiction

How to Hear from God

In Pursuit of Peace

Knowing God Intimately

Seven Things That Steal Your Joy

Any Minute

Secrets to Exceptional Living

Making Marriage Work

Straight Talk on Insecurity

Straight Talk on Loneliness

Straight Talk on Discouragement

Celebration of Simplicity

Don't Dread

How to Hear from God Study Guide

Jesus—Name Above All Names

Life in the Word

Prepare to Prosper

Straight Talk on Depression

Straight Talk on Worry

Teenagers Are People Too

The Power of Determination

The Power of Forgiveness

The Secrets of Spiritual Power

Weary Warriors, Fainting Saints

Beauty for Ashes

Do It Afraid!

Eight Ways to Keep the Devil Under Your Feet

Ending Your Day Right

Enjoying Where You Are on the Way to Where You Are Going

Joyce Meyer Spanish Titles

Pensamientos de Poder

Come la Galleta...Compra los Zapatos

La Revolución de Amor

Empezando Tu Día Bien

Las Siete Cosas Que Te Roban el Gozo

By Dave Meyer

Life Lines

Also Available at Joyce Meyer Ministries

Conversations

I Promise You